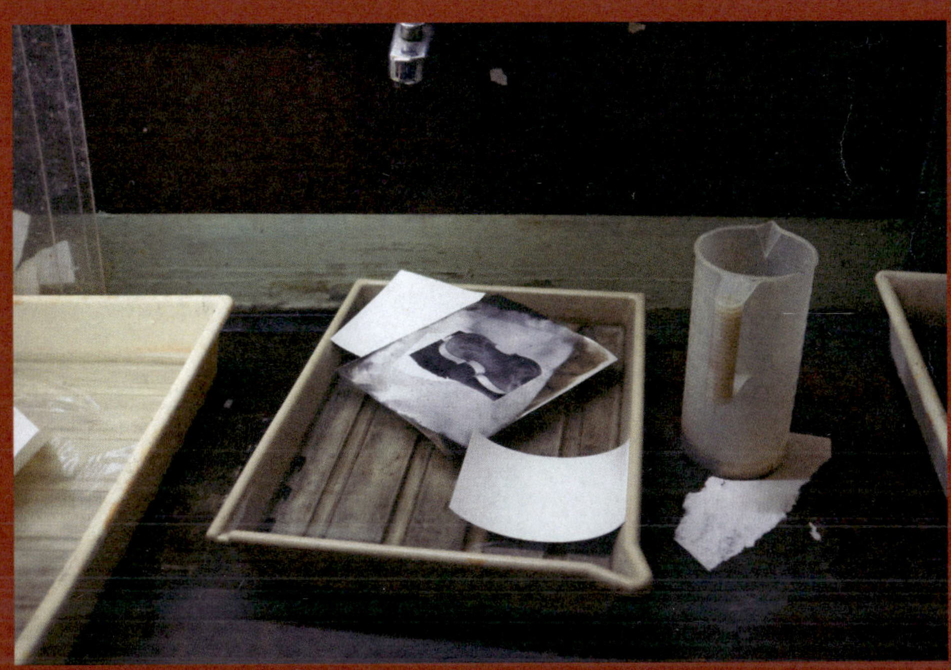

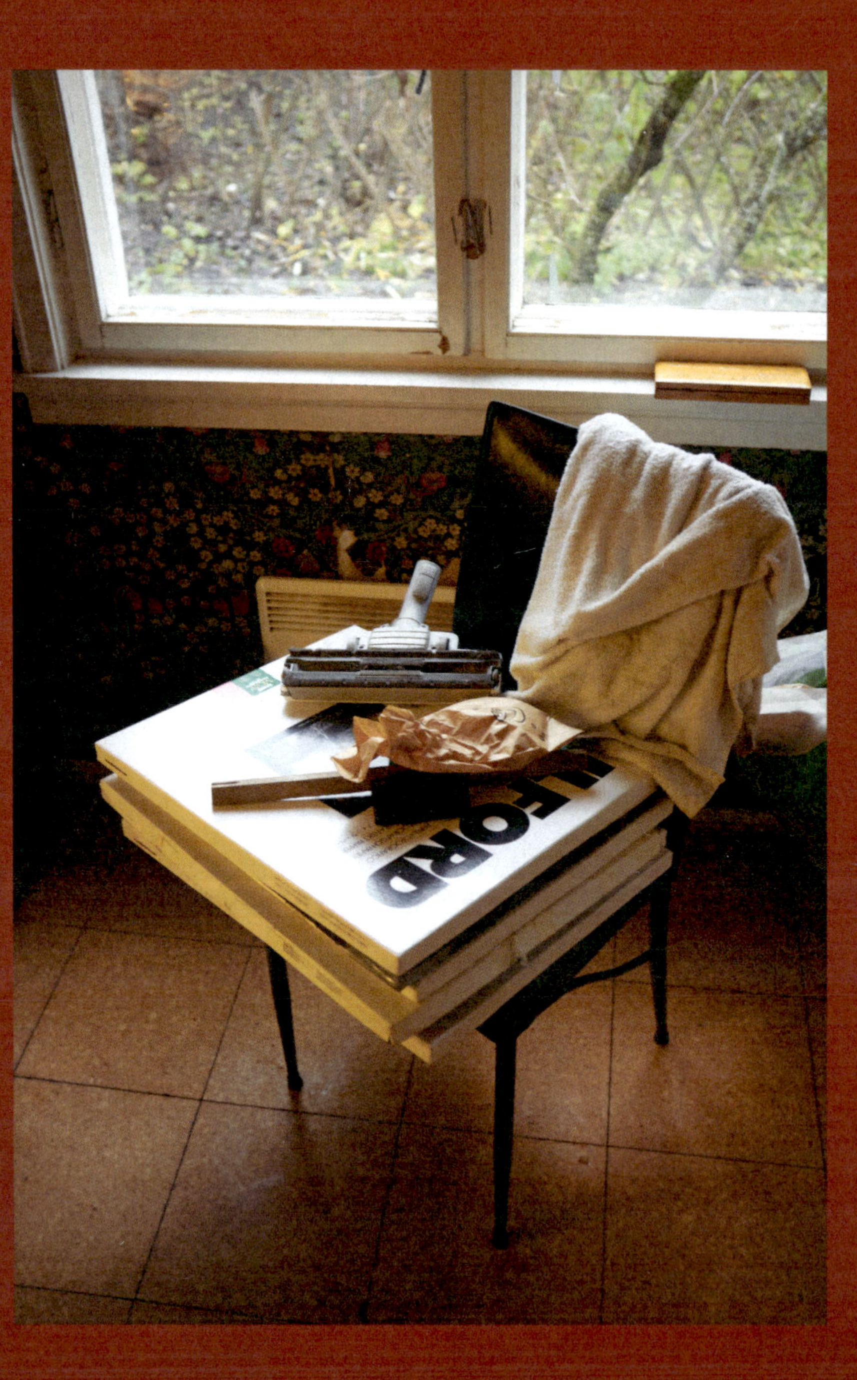

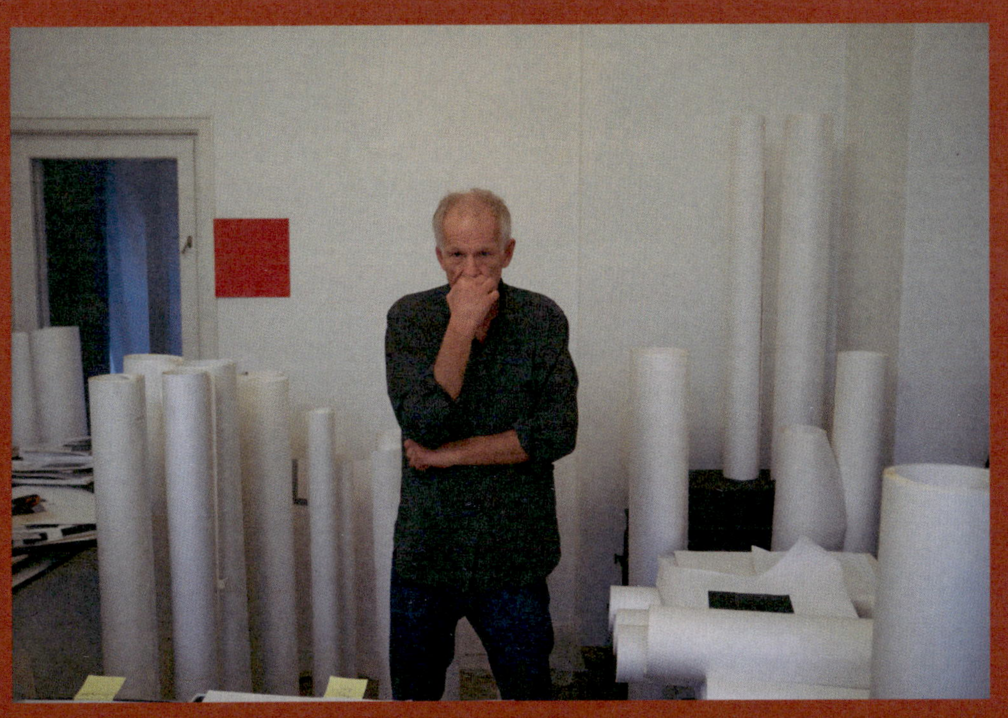

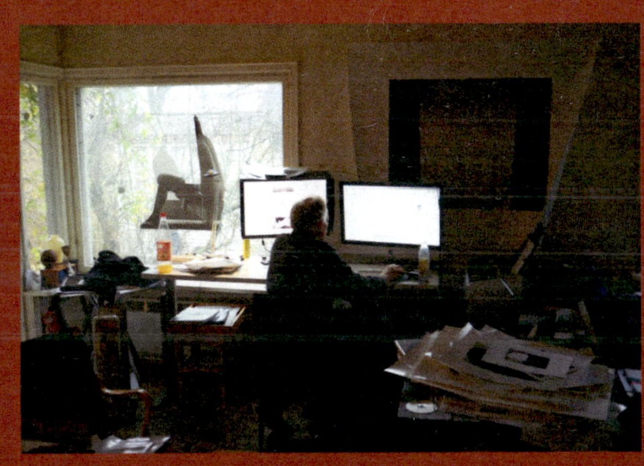

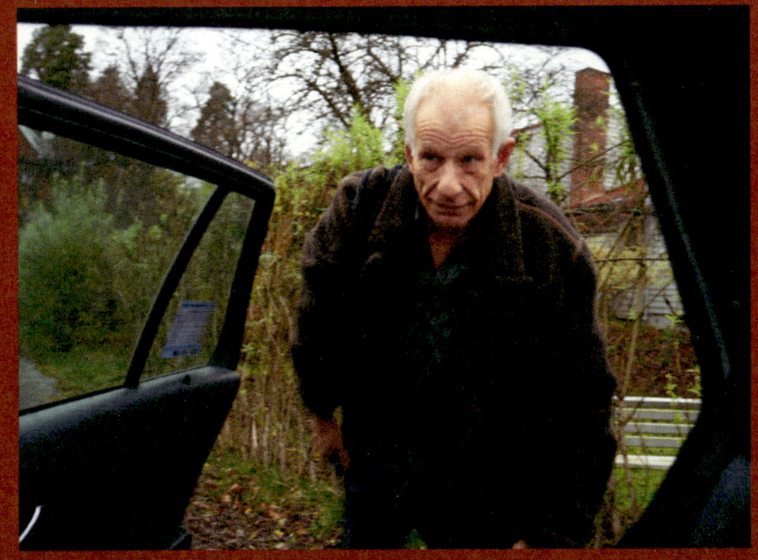

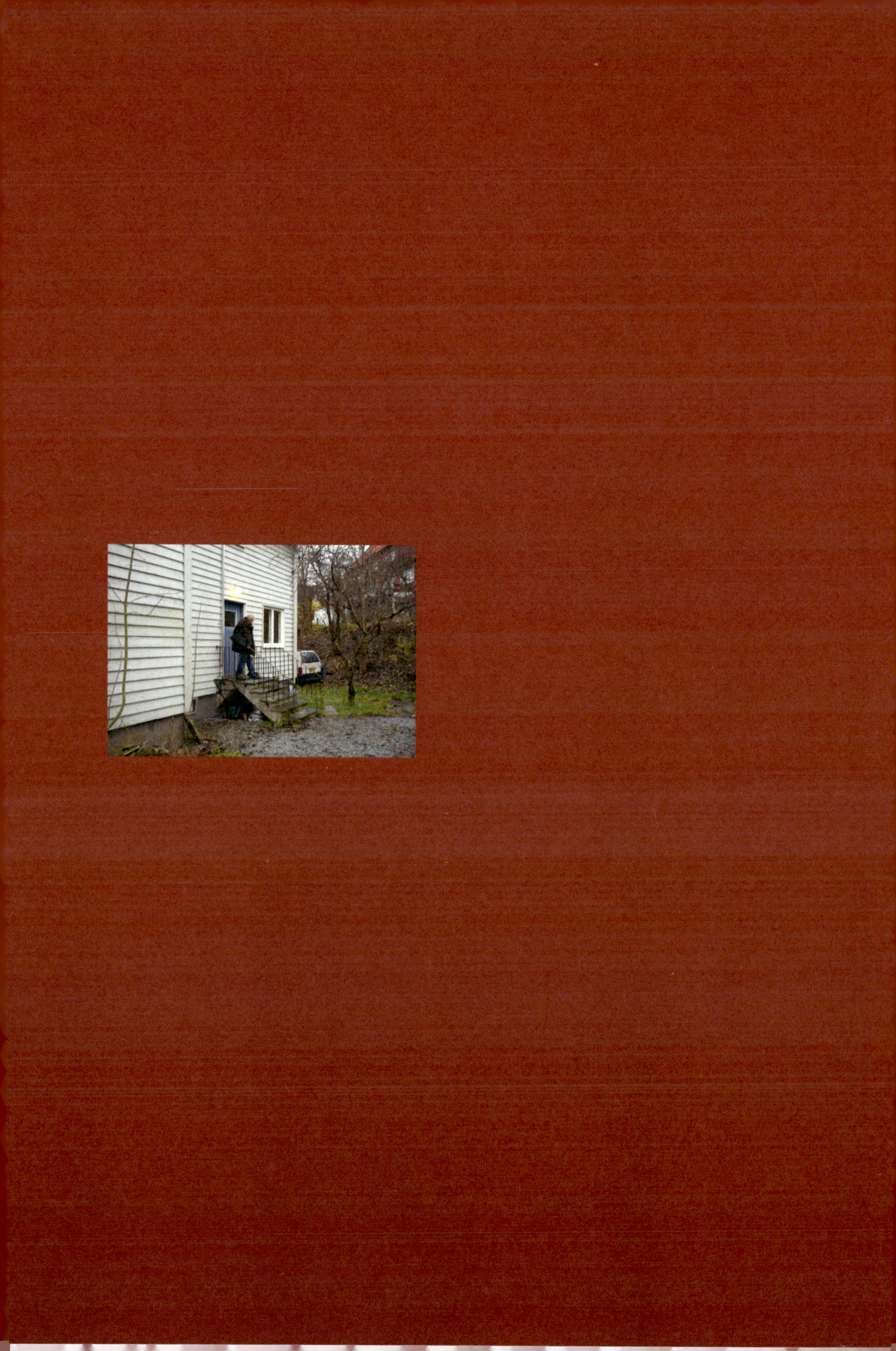

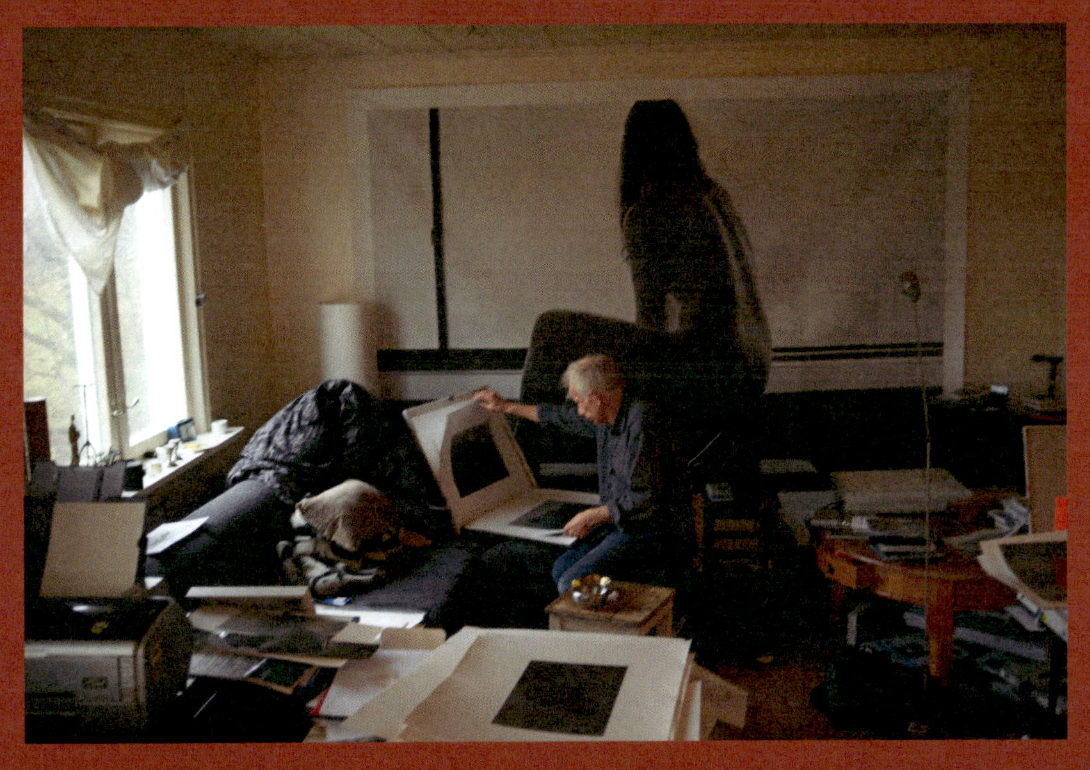

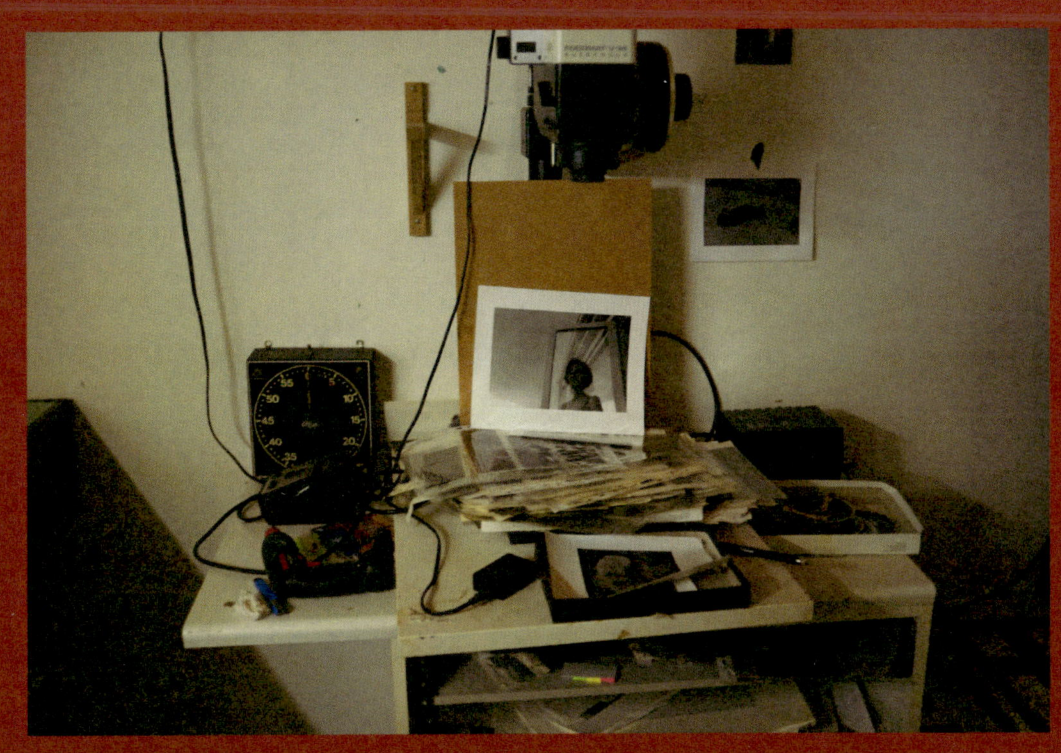

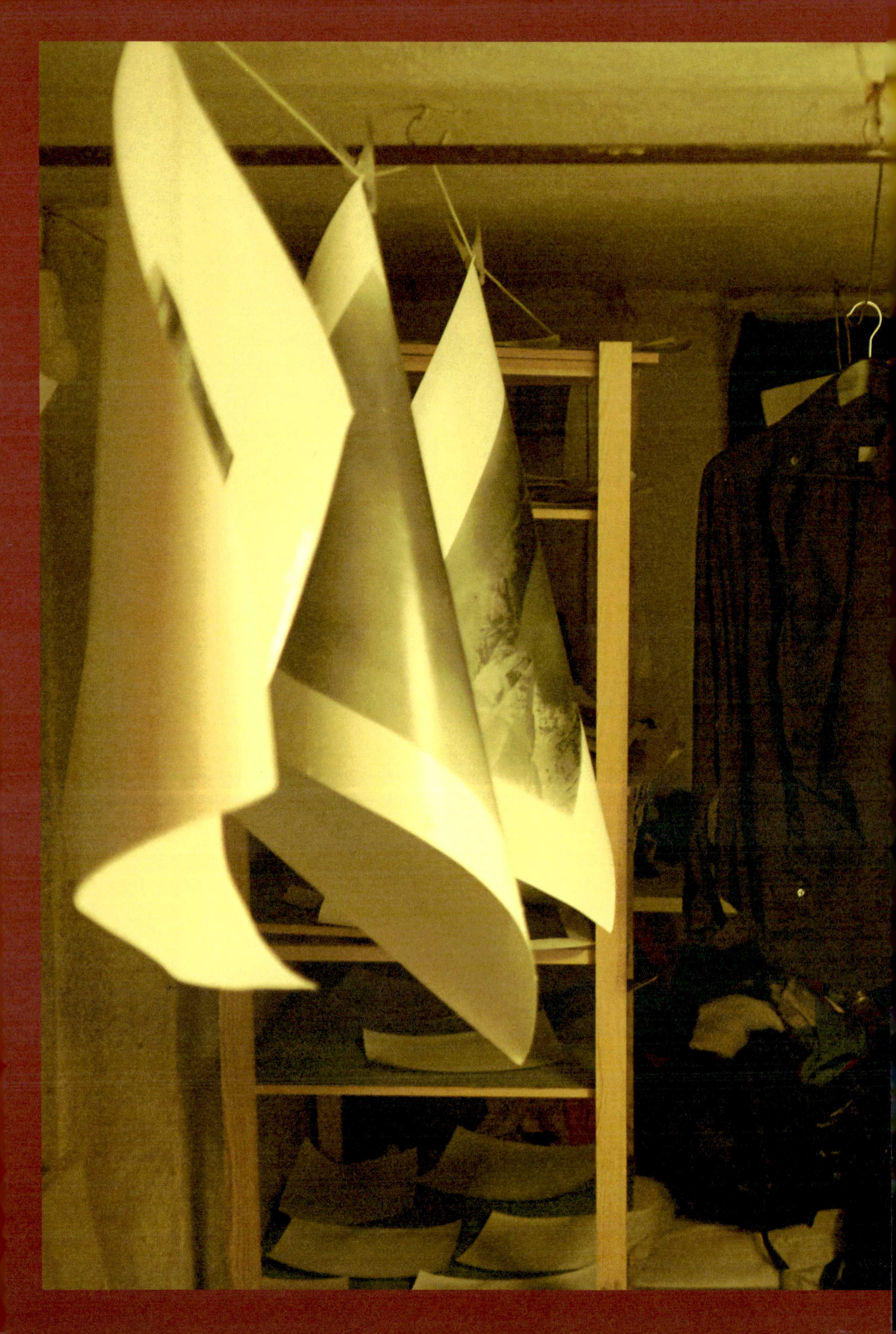

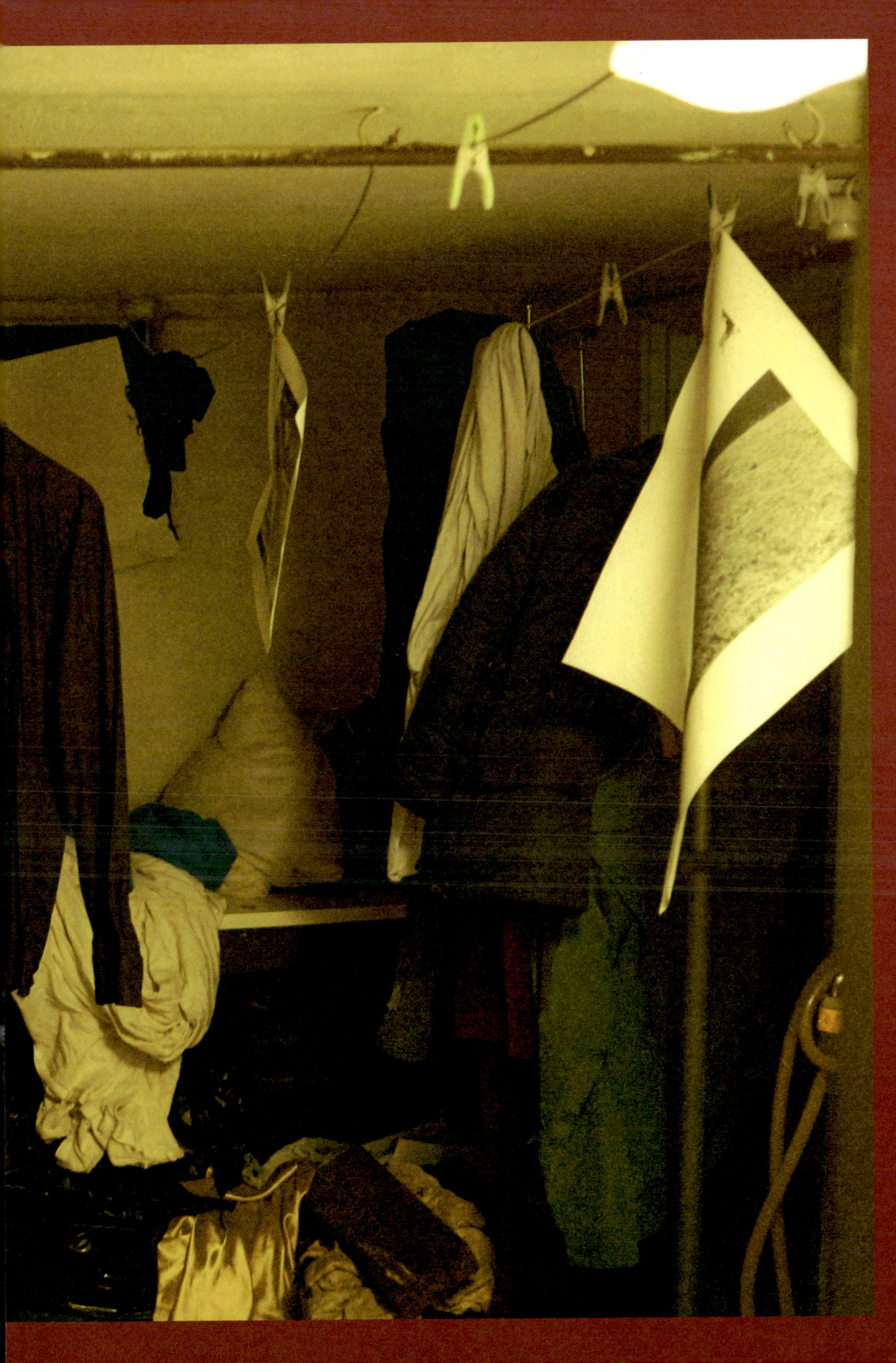

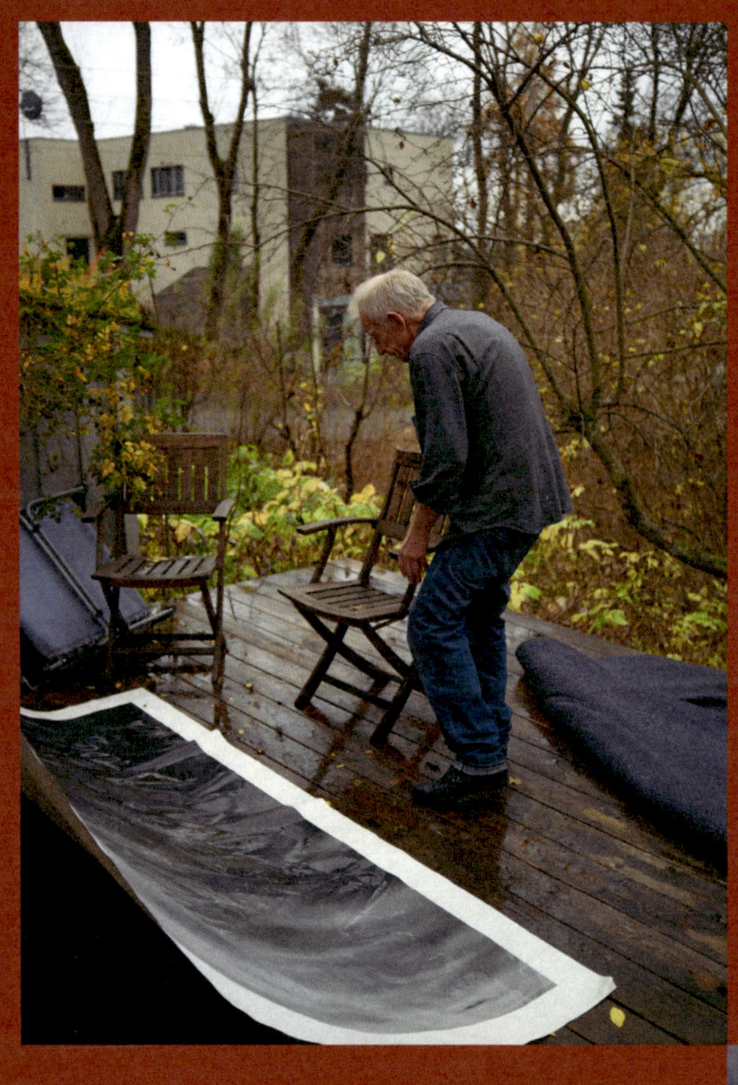

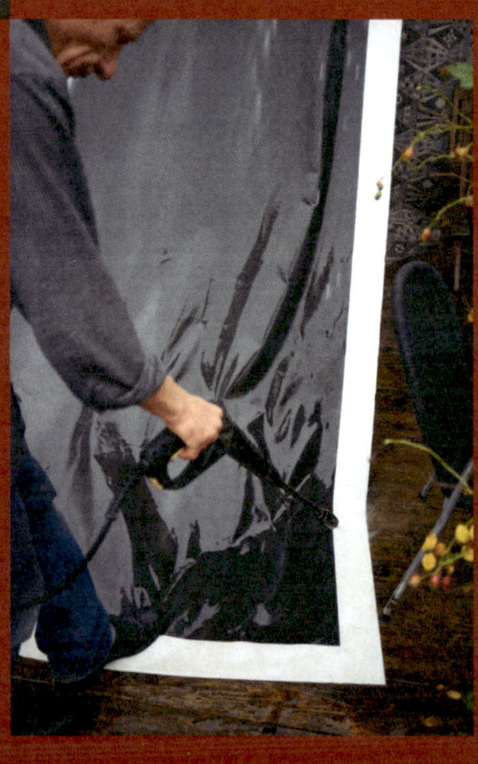

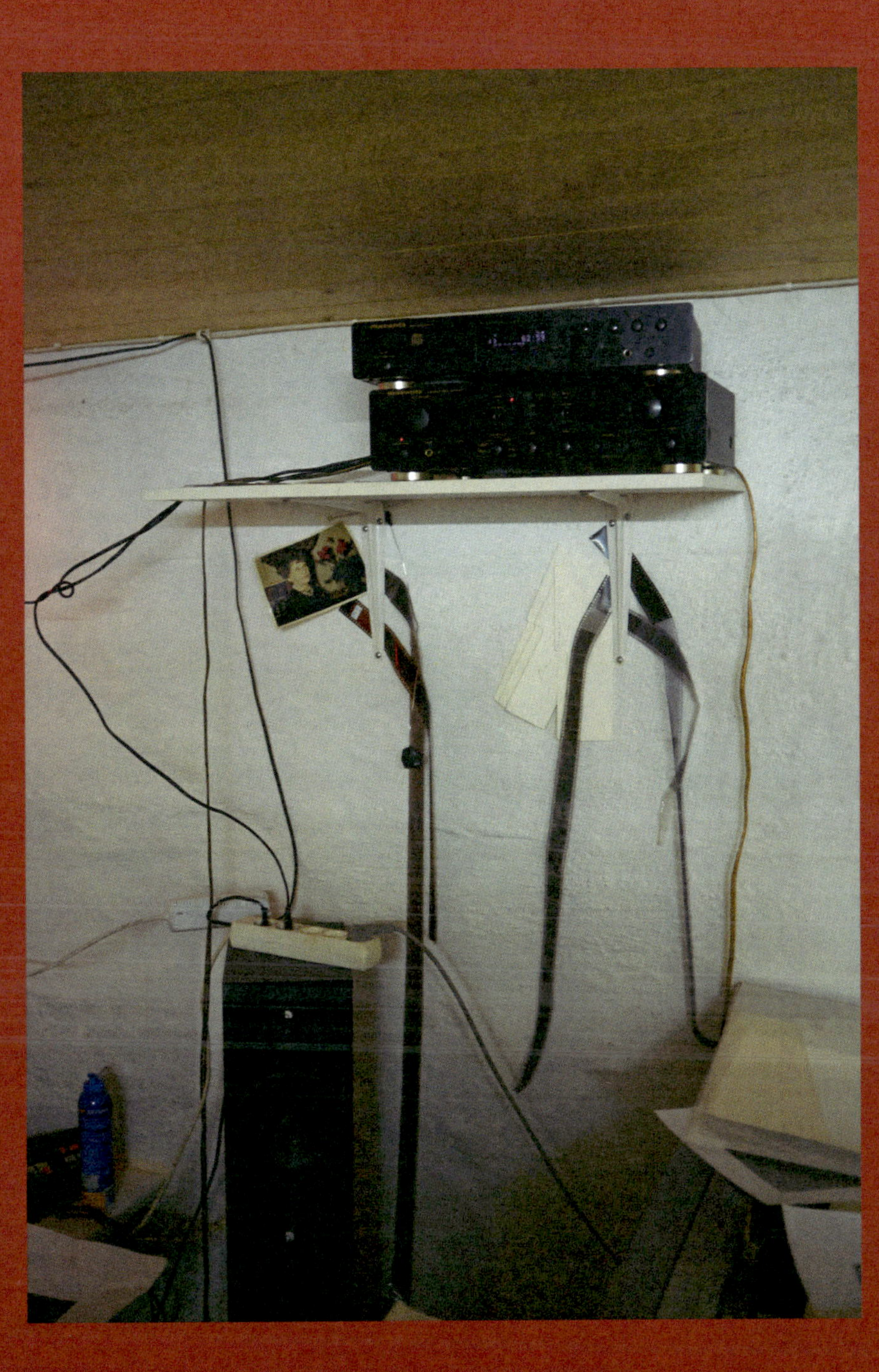

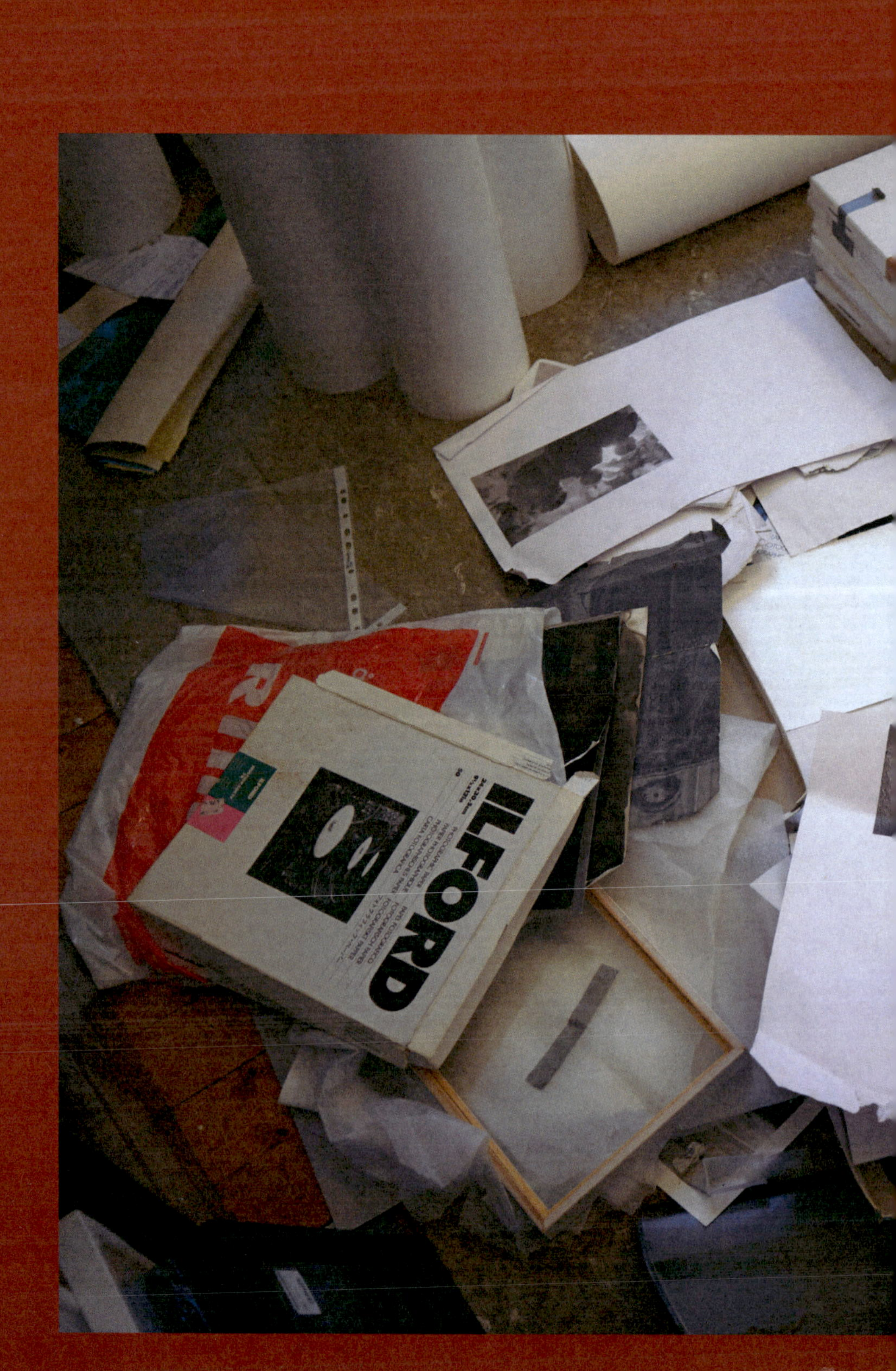

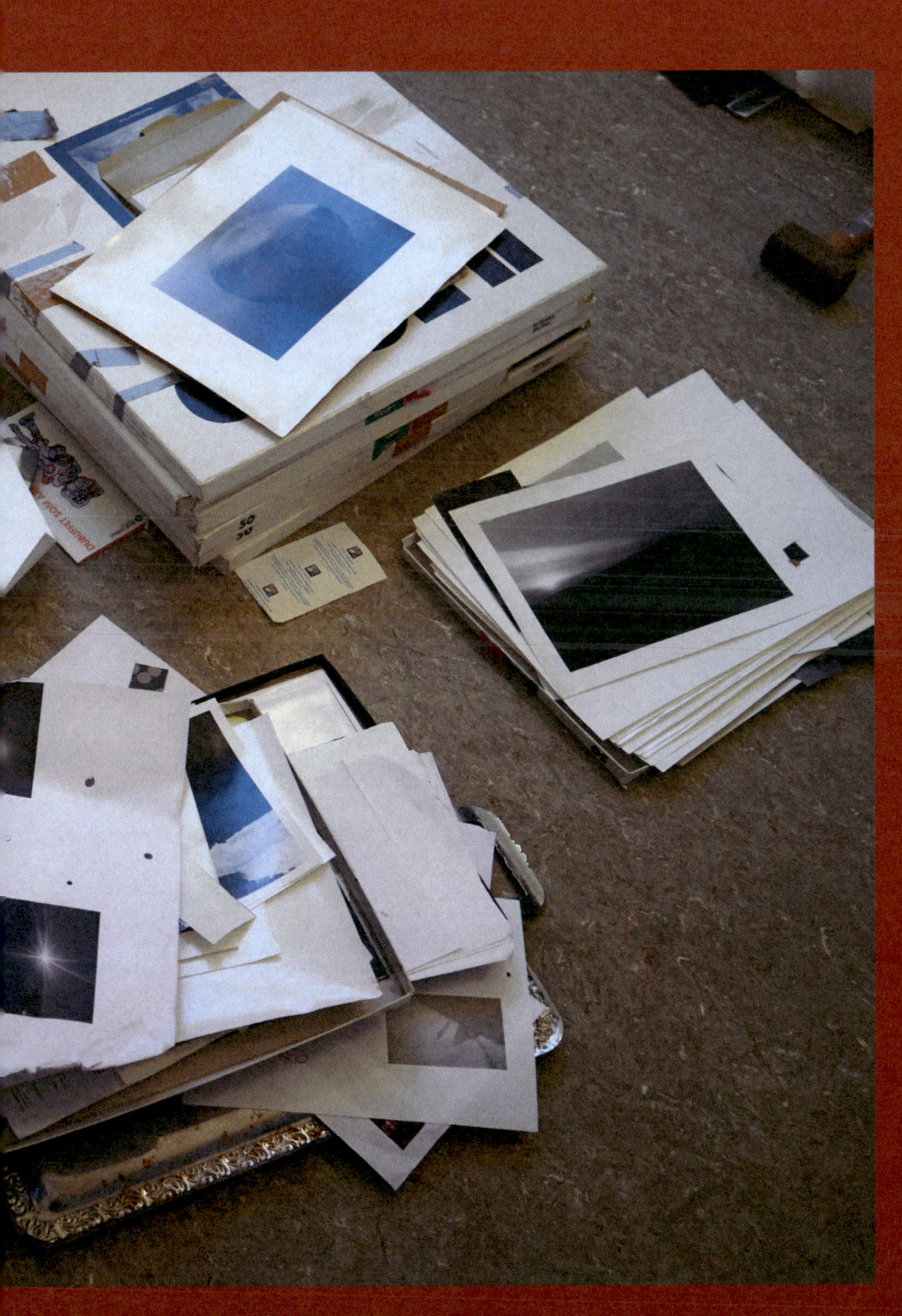

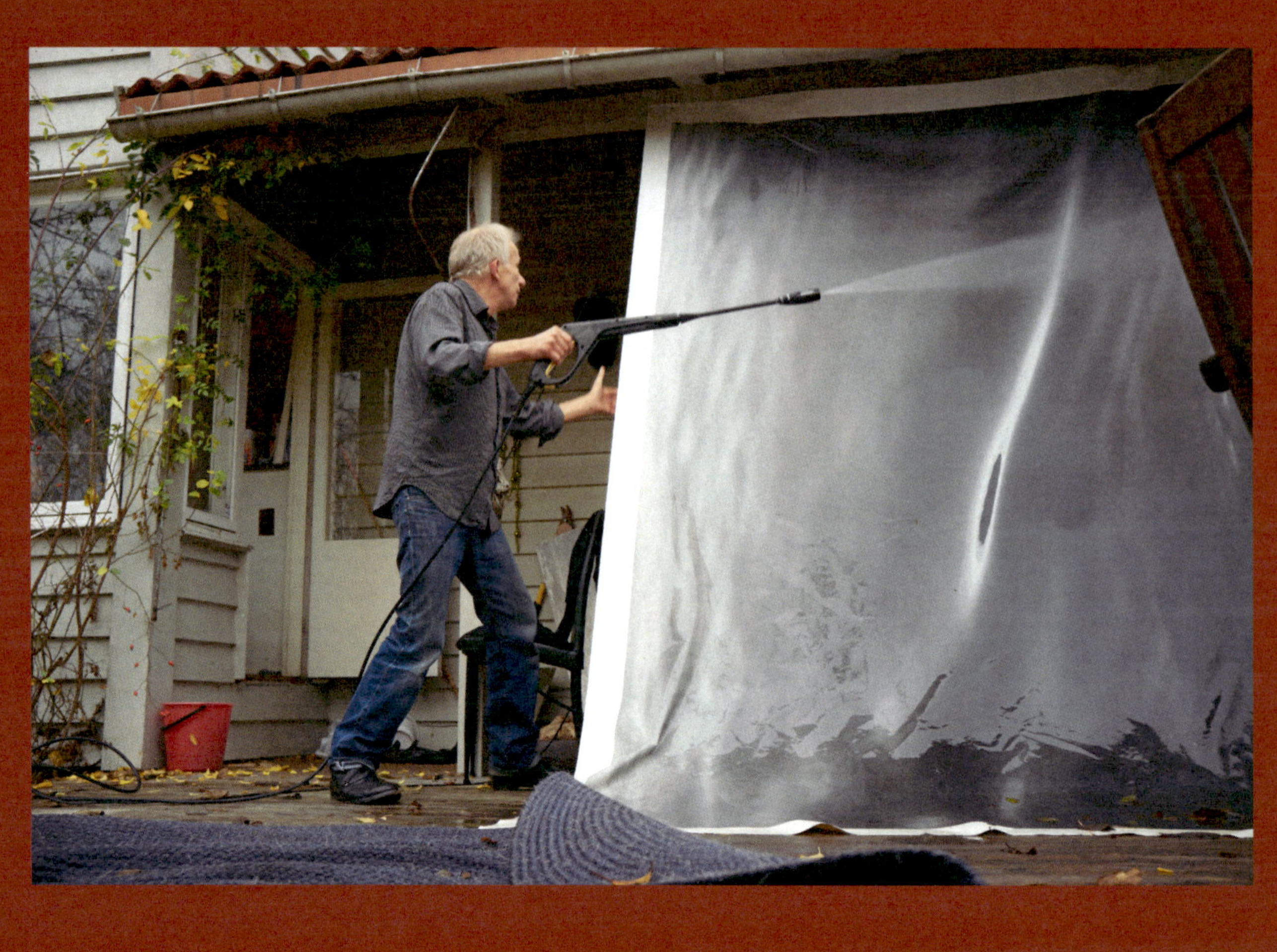

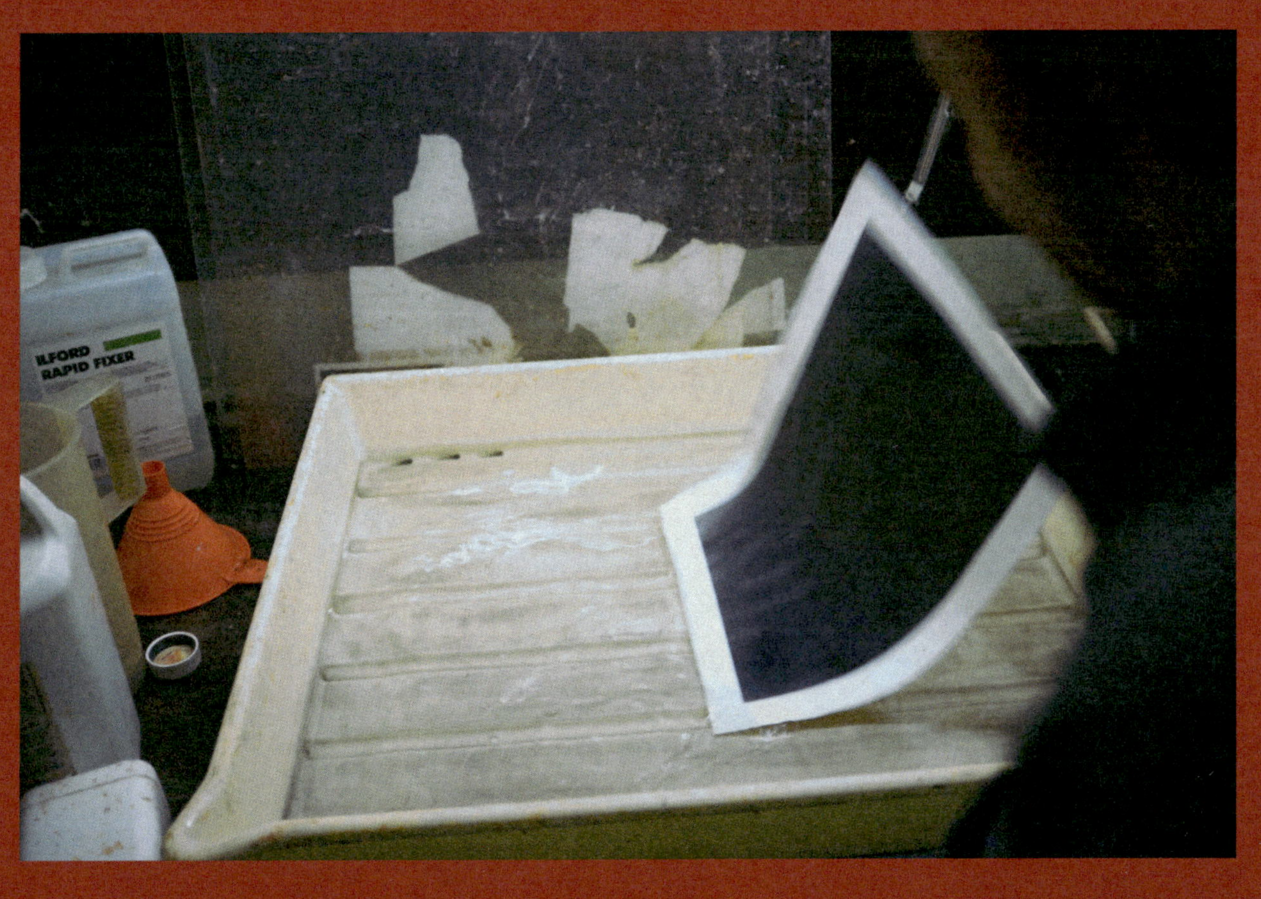

ILFORD
RAPID FIXER

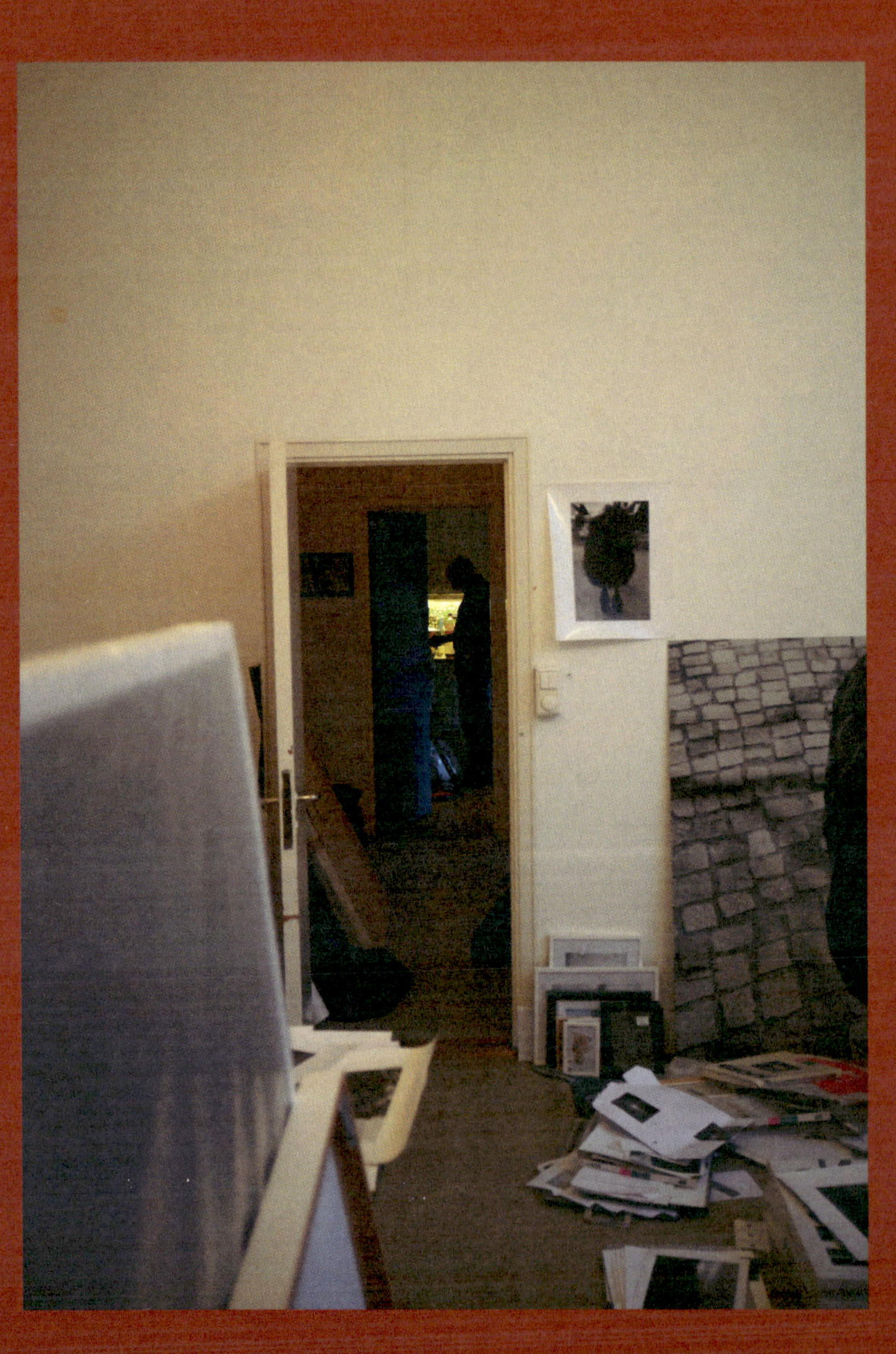

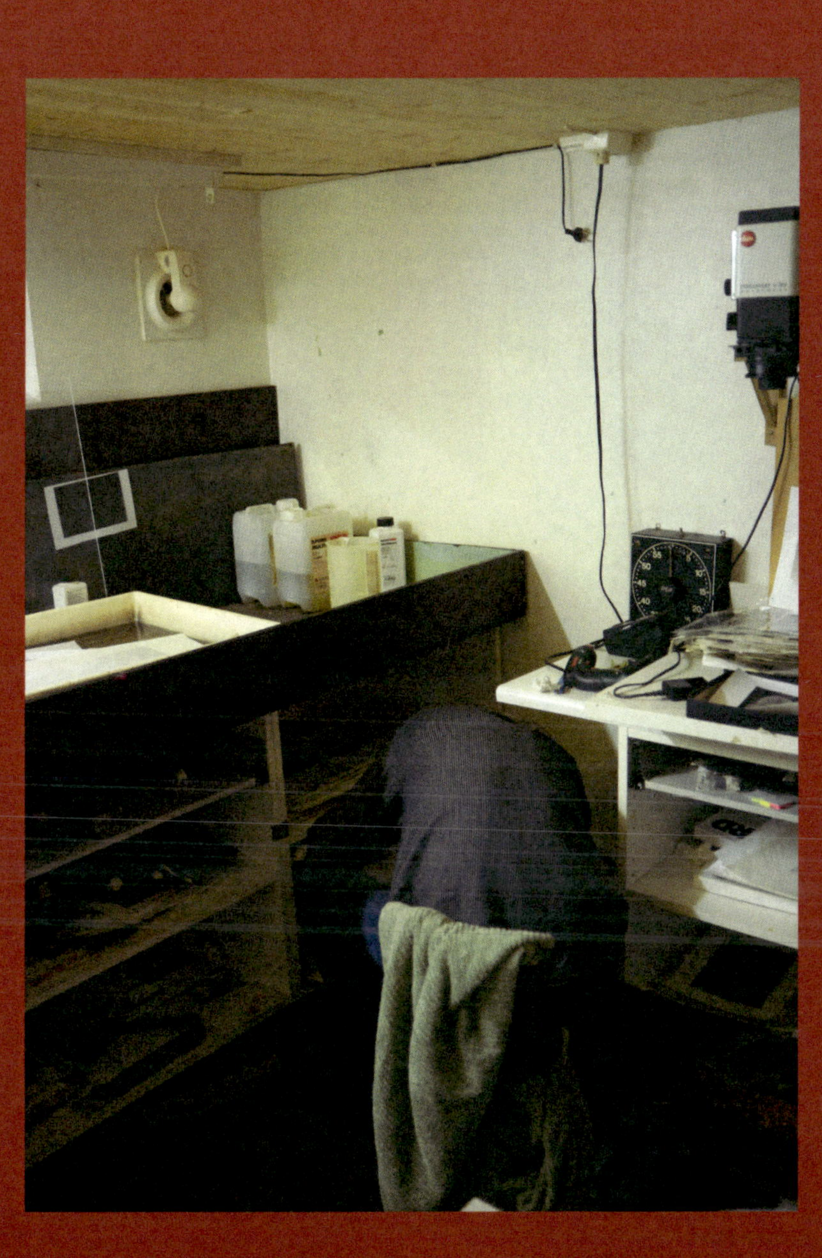

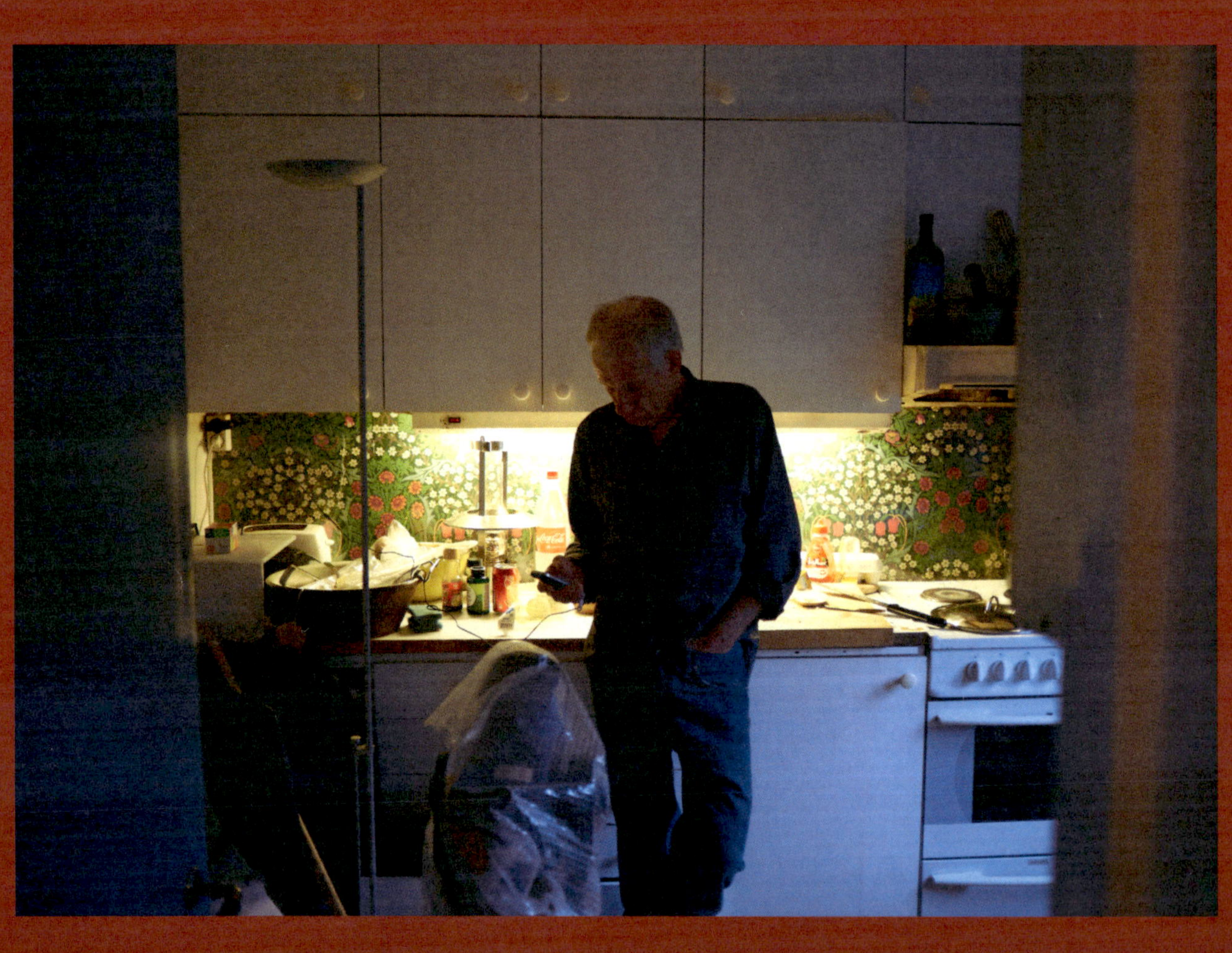

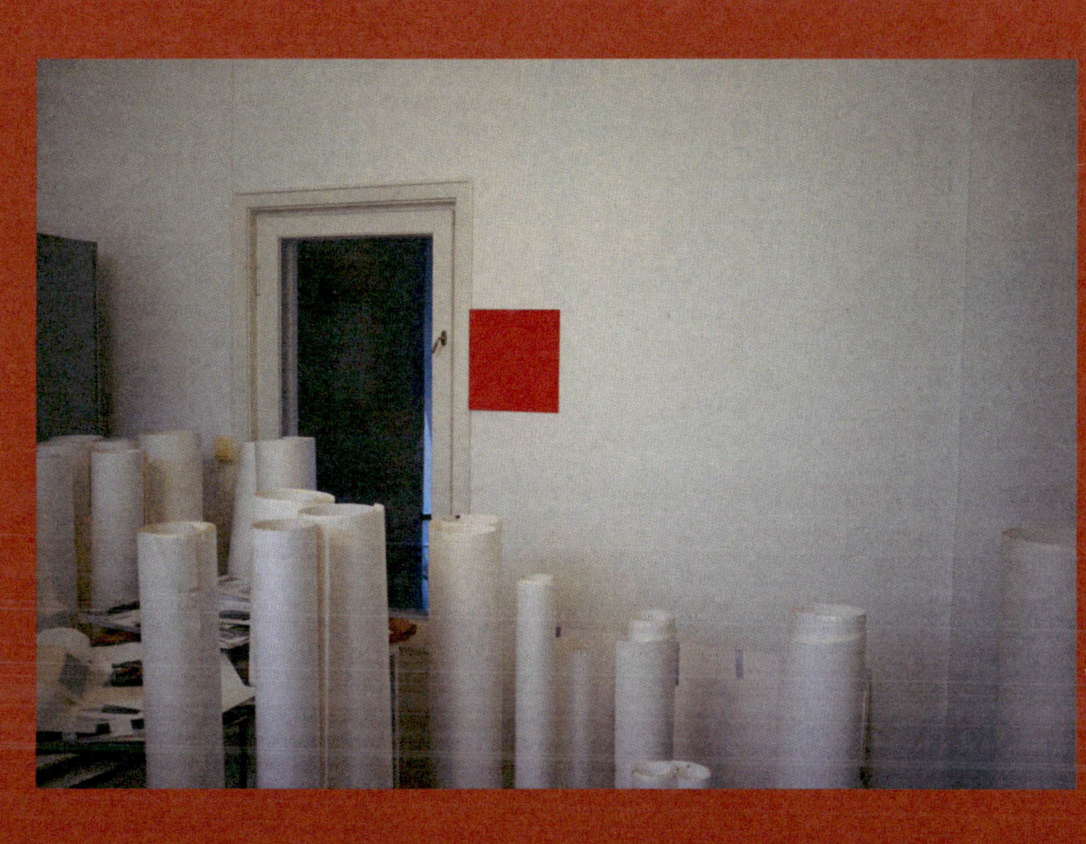

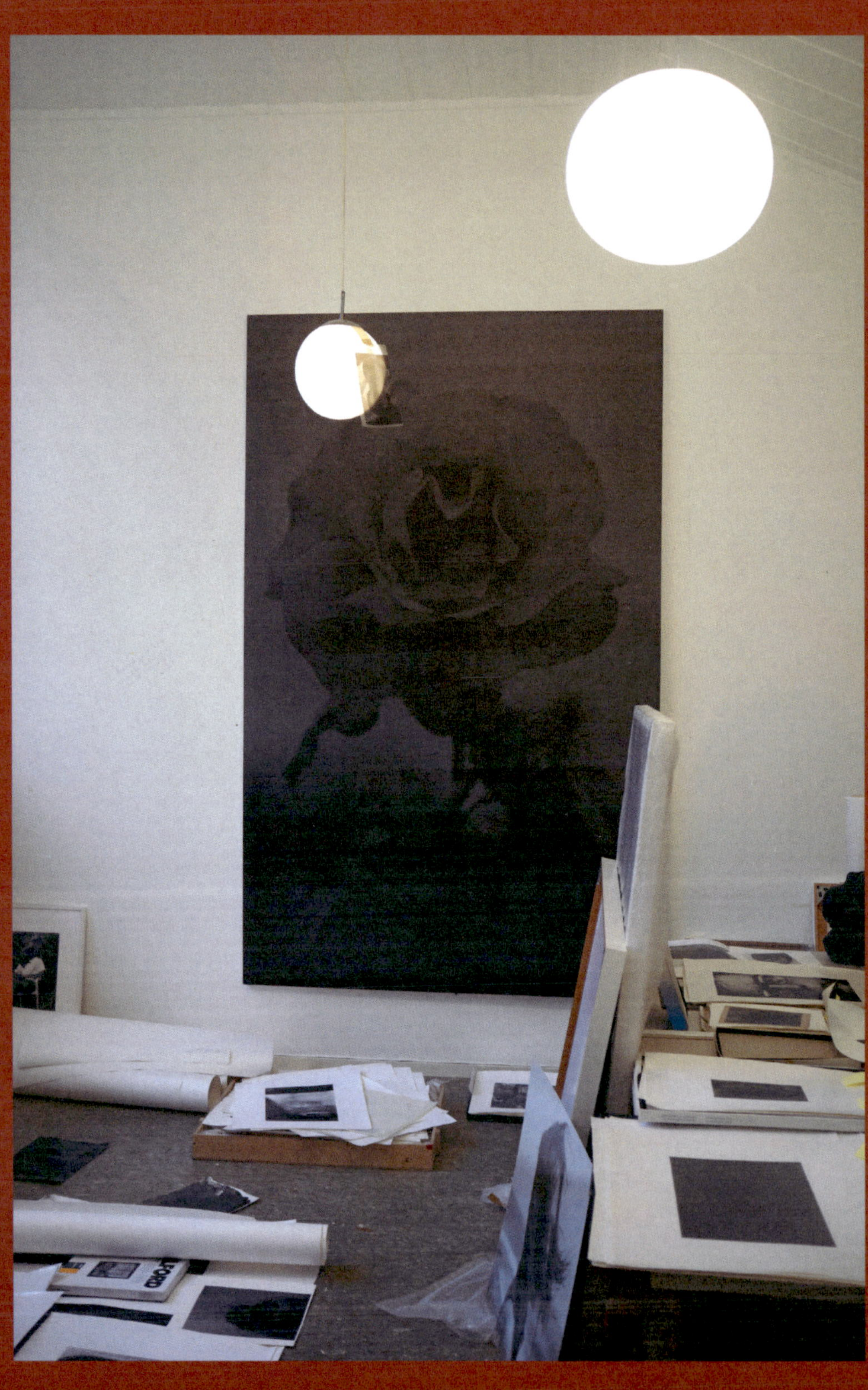

11.11.2011 at 12:26. Oslo. Norway.
Marius W Hansen was photographed
by Tom Sandberg

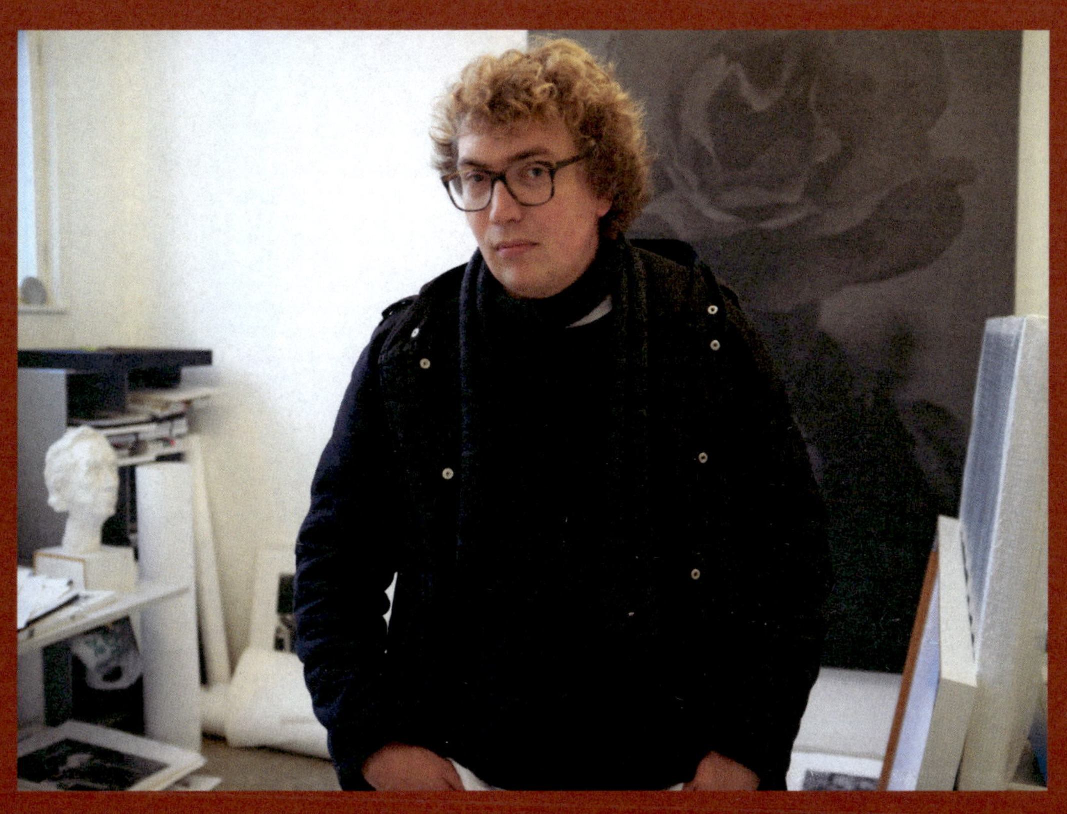

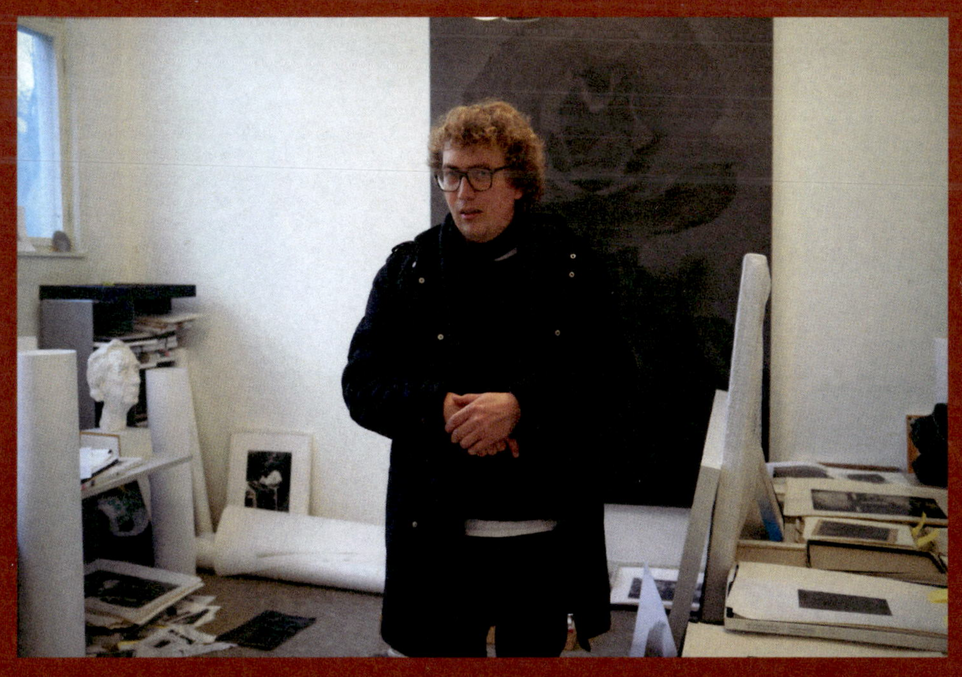

Tom Sandberg

1953 - 2014